Around
Ashby-de-la-Zouch

IN OLD PHOTOGRAPHS

An aerial view looking east along Kilwardby/Market Streets and the Nottingham Road. Most of the fields are, and will be, disappearing under private housing and light industry.

Around
Ashby-de-la-Zouch

IN OLD PHOTOGRAPHS

KENNETH HILLIER

Alan Sutton Publishing Limited
Phoenix Mill · Far Thrupp · Stroud
Gloucestershire

First Published 1994

British Library Cataloguing in Publication Data.
A catalogue record for this book is available from
the British Library.

ISBN 0-7509-0752-5

Typeset in 9/10 Sabon.
Typesetting and origination by
Alan Sutton Publishing Limited.
Printed in Great Britain by
Redwood Books, Trowbridge.

Printing was, apparently, first introduced in
Ashby by Samuel Beadsmoore in 1780. His
printing-press could still be seen at the
firm's premises at 78 Market Street in the
1890s. It survived, in a dilapidated form, in
the basement of the Floral Hall in Bath
Street, until the latter was demolished in
1967.

Contents

The Loudoun Memorial, erected in memory of Lady Edith Maud Hastings, the Countess of Loudoun, and unveiled on Thursday, 24 July 1879.

Introduction

The picture above is possibly the earliest surviving photograph of Market Street. The amateur detective work that goes into dating such views is fascinating in its own right. Holy Trinity still has its spire: it must be earlier than 1900. The building presently occupied by the Midland Bank has not been erected: it is before 1892. H. & E. Bullen have not converted 53 Market Street into a shop: this puts the picture prior to 1881. But the key is the fact that the second shop on the right bears the superscription LOVELL. John James Lovell was in business as a draper in the 1875 Directory; but by 1877 the shop had been taken over by Howe Bros, also drapers and milliners.

Photographs such as these have been preserved by old established families, whose descendants are still living in the town; others have been purchased by amateur collectors; many are picture postcards, which were published in their thousands from the turn of the century, enjoying a heyday before and immediately after the First World War. Much, it is true, survives; but so many buildings – even whole street scenes – have disappeared, usually to the developer or road-widener. It is important that as many of these visual records of the past are preserved and shown to as wide an audience as possible. If one cannot appreciate one's own immediate heritage, which includes an understanding of how it evolved, then one is the poorer for it.

Heavy traffic on Tamworth Road.

SECTION ONE

David and Harry Trevor

Harry Trevor's Castle Studio in Prior Park Road stood just in front of the old toll-house (later nicknamed The Priest's House). Harry stands next to his wife Helen and Mrs Grew from the Lodge.

David Trevor came to Ashby in the late 1870s and built up a great reputation for indoor and outdoor photography. The 1892 *Guide* said he was not only a photographer but an artist.

His son, Harry, established his own photography business in 1899, first at 58a Market Street, then in Prior Park Road, and finally at 20 South Street.

The Trevor family. Standing, left to right: Constance, David, Edith. Sitting: Ida, Mrs Edith Trevor, Elsie. Harry probably took the photograph.

A Trevor view of the girls' schoolroom at North Street School. Hilda Trevor (1907–93), Harry's youngest daughter, is second from left, one row in. Miss Annie Outram is the teacher.

The corner of Brook Street and Market Street from the Trevor camera. Charles Belton, 'brush manufacturer, painter, paper hanger and house decorator', owned the corner shop.

One of several pictures of the 1897 Jubilee, taken by David Trevor. Father and son dominated the period between 1880 and 1914, with a great deal of their work surviving.

SECTION TWO

The Main Routes into Ashby

Mrs Hall (?) outside her cottage on Wilfred Place – once the main road to Tamworth, before the railway line was built.

Lount toll-house at the Staunton–Newbold crossroads. In a derelict state, it was pulled down in the 1930s during road widening. It was the scene of several accidents, one where a car from Newbold crashed into a motor cycle combination from Nottingham. The lady in the side-car was killed.

Ashby workhouse on Nottingham Road (opposite Wykes' Garage). Miss Sandwith (matron in the 1930s – she returned home to Preston when the workhouse closed) with her friend Miss Hurst, of Smisby Road.

The last master, Mr A.V. Smith, with his son Vernon. The workhouse was built as a House of Industry in 1826, and could hold over 300 inmates after enlargement in 1836. It closed in the 1930s and was demolished a decade later.

Many admitted to the workhouse stayed only a night. Often they would leave early the next morning, jumping the hedge to get out of any work and being chased by an irate porter. Alice Pegg stands behind Vernon Smith and next to Martha Bradford (*c.* 1928).

Opposite the workhouse was a post-mill, disused by the mid-1880s but surviving in a dilapidated state into this century. A Scot named Poyser lived there as caretaker in the final years.

Old Park Villas was originally a row of eight houses, built by William Slater, who lived at The Grange in Tamworth Road. He is remembered as a 'terrible stern man' who had three daughters.

The new Girls' Grammar School was opened on Tuesday, 16 September 1902, by the Marquess of Granby, Lord Lieutenant of Leicester. The ceremony cost £61 6s. 6d.; the school building £7,602.

Wood Street Farm was over 300 years old, with beamed ceilings 'still in the shape of the trees that had been cut through the middle', according to Mr and Mrs Bryan, who farmed here between 1941 and 1968. After a three-day chimney fire, part of the roof was taken off to find a fully preserved dovecot underneath.

On the right were two inns: the Bull and the Flaxdressers. The former closed in the mid-1970s and the Flax has changed its name several times since 1982. The Ashby Garage, on the left, is the oldest in the town.

The Leicester Road toll-house stood on the left at the far side of Corkscrew Lane. Dick Britain lived here at the turn of this century. A ghost is said to haunt the lane, ever since a suicide jumped in front of a train at the nearby Black Bridge.

Leicester Road turns sharp left to skirt school property. As long ago as the 1930s, plans existed to carry the road straight on to Nottingham Road. Perhaps the church wall would not have been hit so often if such plans had materialized.

On 30 July 1897 the Cottage Hospital was opened by Earl Ferrers, with Masonic ceremonies. It was mainly funded by Mr and Mrs Edward Ison in honour of the Queen's Jubilee. The hospital contained a male and a female ward, each with five beds and a cot.

On 15 September 1880 the Boys' Grammar (Classical) School moved into these buildings on the corner of Leicester Road.

St Helen's Vicarage was probably on the site of the first Boys' Grammar School (1567) and some plague pits. The three-storey house on the right was once the George III inn.

Wood Street is part of medieval Ashby. Halfway down, on the right, was Grundy's baker's shop, with the bakehouse up the yard. A horsedealer, carrier and bootmaker were some of the inmates of the rest of the row in the late 19th century.

Traffic made a sharp turn left at the bottom of Wood Street. This row is long gone. On the corner was Goadby's printing works. Samuel Taylor, bill poster, lived at No. 1 in 1900.

The Ashby–Tamworth turnpike met three minor roads at Five Lane Ends, where there was a toll-house (demolished since the Second World War).

Leonard Piddocke was to erect a fine mansion off Tamworth Road, but after building this lodge nothing more occurred. For long called Wamba's Lodge, it then became an inn, The Square and Compass, which closed after a lawsuit. It was a farm for years.

Tamworth Road was a 'posh' development of the late 19th/early 20th centuries. Kingsford Osmond ran a boarding and day school for young gentlemen at Victoria Villas in 1870. Thomas Farmer, the assistant overseer, lived at Ivanhoe Villa (built 1876) in 1900.

Station Road was built when the Leicester–Burton railway was laid down in 1848–9. The new road cut across the grounds of the Royal Hotel, depriving it of an extensive garden frontage.

The Royal Hotel (the Hastings Hotel until *c.* 1835–8) was built by Robert Chaplin in 1826–7 as a prestigious family hotel for patrons of the Ivanhoe Baths.

Rawdon Terrace (1822–6), probably also built by Chaplin, serviced the baths as boarding lodgings for 'respectable families'. Dr Kennedy, resident physician to the baths, lived there in the 1830s.

Flora Paulyna Hetty Barbara Hastings, Duchess of Norfolk (d. 11 April 1887), left jewellery to be sold to build a Catholic church in Ashby. Her husband Henry, 15th Duke of Norfolk, sold the jewels and built this church in honour of the Blessed Virgin Mary, under the invocation of Our Lady of Lourdes.

The main road for Burton used to go up Kilwardby Street and along Hill Street (Rosemary Lane in 1768), where there were four blocks of cottages. Only two now survive – the nearest went between the wars.

Kilwardby Street once stretched to the present War Memorial. The Water Tower (1852) has not been used since the early 1900s. The top of the street was known as The Hill. Fisher's solicitors have practised from the building on the right for well over a century.

'Knock-em-down' (F.W.) Jones of Woodville was a familiar sight in the 1960s – here he prepares to demolish Boundary Congregational Church. The toll-house is the last standing near Ashby.

Burton Road Hill was too steep for horse-drawn traffic and was known as Clap Lane. The Burton and Ashby Light Railway was routed by the Council to pass on the side of the terraces, not the villas.

The Blue and Green Coat School (Lower Church Street) and the English School were merged after a critical Inspector's Report in 1907. A new Council School was opened on 9 January 1911, in New Burton Road. W.E. Jennings, the first head, died in office in 1923. J.W. Jackson was head from 1923 to 1953.

The Garden of Eden in the process of demolition. Sally Cuckoo, 'who would never face anybody', lived there. Ortons built a pair of houses on the site.

A tramcar travels along Derby Road. To its right, Parker opened a garage in the 1920s, which was extended when the cinema, built next to it in the same decade, was closed on 31 December 1963.

Derby Road from Market Street. William Aldred Haynes (established 1841) was a baker and grocer; on the right, Abraham Baxter and Sons were tailors and woollen drapers (and postcard sellers). Both were demolished to make way for the Light Railway.

SECTION THREE

The Minor Routes into Ashby

Carriages like this were used by the great houses to meet passengers from the railway station. This one draws breath along Willesley Lane.

A delightful rural view of Willesley Lane, near Valley Farm – no white lines or kerbs in those days. The high bank to the left marks the course of the Ticknall railroad.

Smisby Road, with its Edwardian terraces on the right and fields to the left. The first council houses were built there, at North Town, in 1921.

William Smedley, the Ashby postmaster, with his herd of cows. His field is now occupied by United Biscuits, but the house on the right still stands.

The Callis was described in 1837 as follows: 'The houses were poor, the roadway an open sewer, and the women old hags, half clothed, loud in speech and rough in manner.' Needless to say, all has changed since then.

C.B. Parsons' car faces an opponent in a bet that they could not pass each other under the Callis Bridge. After the Second World War the bridge took only 45 minutes to demolish.

Tradition has it that the cottage on Hill Street corner was once a chapel. Outlines of its lancet windows could still be seen in 1907. Bob Parker lived there in the early 20th century. The cemetery keeper, Mr Grainger, lived opposite.

The first toll on Lower Packington Road was taken on 6 April 1843. Here, Sarah Matilda Price (d. 1926 aged 74) stands by the gate, c. 1907. A well for the lodge was behind the fence.

Until very recently green fields still stretched beyond the railway line, with ridge and furrow clearly visible.

Housing now obscures the view to the castle. Mount Walk remains much the same. The school fields to the right were known as Far and Near Mount Close; they all got their names from the Mount House – the triangular fort built in the Civil War.

Bath Street

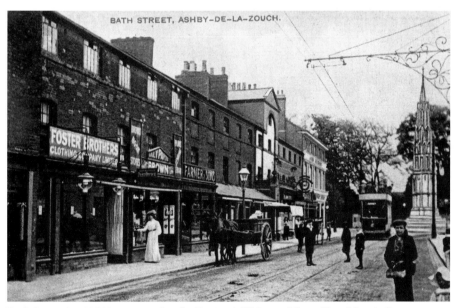

BATH STREET, ASHBY-DE-LA-ZOUCH.

Bath Street (*c.* 1822) was previously Cotton Mill Lane. The mill, with a bell tower over its centre, extended from No. 3 to No. 11 and provided employment for thirty to forty girls, often from the Union. Joseph Wilkes of Measham set up the industry.

Two views of the north-west corner of Bath Street, before and after demolition in June 1905. Scott (1907) thoroughly applauded the removal of such 'wretched rookeries'. One man remembers labourers using ropes to pull whole sides of buildings down.

The Ashby Co-op Stores were there from the early 1890s. Beyond, from the right (in 1900), were John Hunt (basket maker), Abraham Chadwick (refreshment house), Joseph Toon (fishmonger), John Sweet (butcher), and Thomas Williscroft (boot and shoe maker).

Dereliction – awaiting demolition by Slater's.

Previously, the corner building was run by John Holdron, ironmonger, who had taken over from William Austin, also an ironmonger. The latter can be traced back to 1855, when he was described as a 'tinman and brazier'.

The Hare and Hounds still stands – just. The Bryans ran the inn from the 1820s until the 1870s. The umbrella sign marks Hezekiah 'Gypsy' Boswell's shop – scissor grinder and umbrella repairer. He appears to have vanished when the building did.

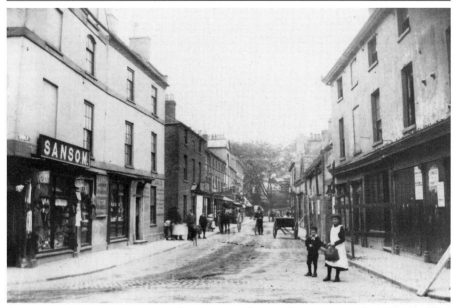

A view south, *c.* 1904. Sansom's hardware and general stores was where the shopper 'could get anything. There was a long counter, and the shop was full of stuff but not untidy'. Mr Wells had a rag and bone business in the opening behind Sansom's.

A view north to the Shoulder of Mutton, where 'Eadie's Fine India Pale and Mild Ales and Wines and Spirits of the finest quality' were available for the 1887 Jubilee. The clock on the right marks Stotts, the jeweller. The Hare and Hounds is on the left.

This row marked the start of Station Road; the site is now a tool hire firm. The little shop was kept by Miss Trussell in around 1900. Above, the Misses Emma, Eleanor and Elizabeth Richards plied their trade as dressmakers.

Edward Louch carried on his carriage, coach-building and wheelwright's business next to his home (demolished *c.* 1938). Foundations were laid for a cinema on the site, but the Second World War intervened and Eric Bailey's car business was built instead.

Where the Loudoun Memorial stands there used to be a clump of trees, west of which there was a spring known as Gawby's Hole (actually, Perrin's Well), because of the gabbling women who stood around it waiting to fill their buckets with water. Holy Trinity spire can be seen in the left distance.

Behind the Memorial was the Saline Baths Infirmary (from 1854) – a charity for the poor. Holdron's took it over in the 1890s.

The double doors led to the Floral Hall, once the Theatre Royal, built in 1828. Successively used by Beadsmoore's and George Brown who were printers, it was demolished in September 1967. Harry Onions, then his daughter Aggie, ran the grocer's shop. Radford's – formerly Francis Bott's – had a café on the ground floor and a tea-room upstairs. Between the wars a three-course lunch was 2s. 6d., but 2s. 3d. to regulars.

SECTION FIVE

Market Street

Hextall's famous frontispiece to his 1852 *History*, 'representing Ashby's main street, wide and well built will give the stranger a fair idea of the external appearance of its chief thoroughfare'.

First left is Haynes the grocers, then the narrow entrance to Derby Road and Baxter's the tailors and hosiers, then Charles Wykes' shop. The huge sign above proclaims the arrival of Holdron's in Market Street, since the 1890s.

The scar caused by the widening of Derby Road survived until 1986, when both Wykes' (now part of Holdron's) and Holdron's were pulled down. Beyond Holdron's is Cash & Co., boot and shoe manufacturers.

Charles Leonard ('little') Wykes, fancy goods dealer and haberdasher. He previously had his shop in the 'island', in the middle of Market Street, at 36a. He moved to 11 Market Street when Ellen Osborne, also a fancy goods dealer, closed in *c*. 1899.

John Holdron, with Ison's, was one of the two great names in hardware and agricultural machinery in Ashby. His West End shop was a veritable emporium of goods.

The London Central Meat Co. later became Grainger's, then Dewhurst's – all butchers.

The Star Supply Stores at 31 Market Street evokes the aura of shopping in the early years of this century. It changed to Melia's and then the International Stores (now Victoria Wine).

This site has seen three buildings this century, the ugliest being the last. From the right: no. 10 – Joseph Kerby (fruiterer); no. 12 – Arthur Dolman (fried fish); no. 14 – William Farmer (fruit seller); Court no. 8 lay down the passage (now Rushton's Yard).

The building that replaced it. Gilbert's boot shop (for a short while, Holloway's removal firm) and Haynes' grocers, from the Derby Road entrance. The building was about to be demolished.

J. & E. Ison (whose plough it is) is just off to the left, 'ironmongers, nail manufacturers, licensed gunpowder and cartridge magazines and agricultural implement dealers'. They were also motor agents for Maxwell and Rover cars by the 1920s.

A parade outside the King's Head. On the right was the New George Inn, in the Measures family's hands from the 1820s to the 1860s.

Thomas Litherland, china dealer, had a shop from *c.* 1830 at 19 Market Street. It had moved by the 1890s to no. 49, where it stayed till it closed in 1957. By 1898 the business included 'china and glass merchants, lawn tennis and fishing tackle, outfitters, ladies' and gentlemen's hairdressing rooms'.

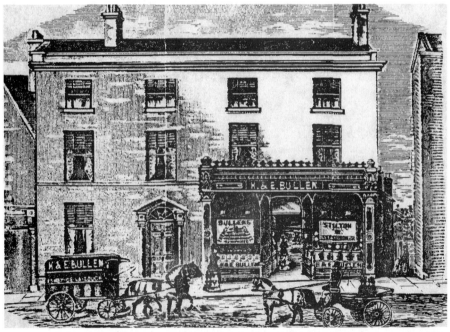

Henry and Ebenezer Bullen were established in business in Ashby by their father in 1872. In 1881 they moved from 66 to 53 Market Street. The firm ceased trading in 1978.

Apothecaries Hall was built on the site of Dr Thomas Kirkland's house in 1868, by Charles Matthews. Next to his chemist's and candlemaker's shop was William Elliott's (stationers) – later Charles Hussey's; the Bull's Head (run by Thomas Dolman in 1892, the year of the photograph); and then Chatterton Bros (grocers).

A view from the top of Market Street. Few dogs would dare walk the street alone today.

William Stanley outside his 'cycle,
perambulator and mail cart depot' at 92
Market Street. The entrance to Court no. 18
is to the right.

In 1900 brothers Harry and Joe Haynes'
cycle and wheelwright's business was at 11
Kilwardby Street. By 1904 Joe was at 83
Market Street; he moved again, to the top
end (now demolished).

Transport

What is there to smile about?

Mr Quinney used to fetch and carry chinaware and other items from Ashby Station to Litherland's, as well as running a general service between villages such as Measham and Oakthorpe.

Mr Broadhurst with Blossom outside Mr Boss' photography studio in Derby Road. Ernest and Hector Smedley, the cart's owners, were builders, contractors and undertakers.

Cutter's horse and cart (decked out for some sort of celebration) outside the Jetty in Tamworth Road. There were several Cutters in business at the turn of the century.

Possibly a fancy dress outing in Bath Street in the 1930s.

A (steam) road train outside Thomas Poole's corn and flour dealers (no. 21) and
S. Hilton & Son (no. 23), bootmakers, in Market Street.

A steam engine accident on Burton Road, opposite Hill Street.

A car was first used at a wedding in Ashby when Ernest Smedley married Elizabeth Ward Poyser, in September 1906. The wedding was at the Primitive Methodist Chapel, New Burton Road.

A 1920 St Helen's Church choir outing, including Ernest Taylor, Joe Curtis, Ted Downs, Canon Sawyer (1906–23), Mr Everett, W. Ison, S. Parkes and Supt Lockton.

J.S. Plant's Removal and Storage firm guaranteed delivery 'to any part of England in 48 hours' in 1920. D. Plant is by the cab.

A Burton and Ashby tram outside the Royal Hotel. The last cars ran into Swadlincote depot on 19 February 1927.

This Leicester-bound train is pulled by a pair of Midland 2–4–0s (early 1890s?). Ashby station was closed to passengers on 7 September 1964, a victim of Beeching's blood-stained axe.

The derelict Derby line platform. Passenger service ended in September 1930 and the line was lifted in 1955.

Road-hog, 1920s-style!

Jubilees and Special Occasions

The Primitive Methodist float in the 1911 Coronation procession. 'Queen of the Roses' is led by Bill Whetton.

'A halt is sounded in the widest part of Market Street, just beyond the western extremity of the lines of dining-tables to form a square . . . the bands are in the centre . . . and the massive harmony of the patriotic hymn ascends to the vaulted blue of heaven's firmament' (J.F. Brazier, describing the 1887 Jubilee celebrations).

'Four arches were erected in appropriate positions, each symbolising some important feature of Her Majesty's reign . . . the one at the western end was named the "Progress Arch", and was intended to represent the progress of material science during the last fifty years' (Brazier, 1887).

'The width of the street allowed of tables, in rows of three, being set down one side for the dinner and tea, and of a double row of Venetian masts on the other side' (Brazier, 1887).

Again the Volunteers played a central part in the celebrations, 'firing a *feu de joie*, the sharp crack of rifles running down the front rank, and up the rear. . .' (1897 Jubilee).

The 1902 Coronation celebrations (or is it the end of war celebrations in 1919?) may have had less spent on street decorations, but were no less enjoyed.

The entrance to Derby Road, bedecked in 1902 with a 'God Save the King' archway.

A view from the other side, which shows Ashby did not forget Queen Alexandra.

The north side of Wood Street, decorated for the 1902 Coronation.

A crowded Market Street salutes George V's Coronation in 1911. Mr Haynes, the grocer, is the bearded man facing the camera.

The head of the 1911 procession reaches the top of Market Street. Evans' shop is on the extreme right.

A good view of the top end of Market Street in 1911.

Kilwardby Street played its part in the 1911 festivities. The level crossing gates can be seen beyond the Midland Hotel.

A crowded Station Road watches the procession pass.

The police station, built in 1862 for £2,000, was enlarged in 1879 to include a magistrates' room and homes for a superintendent and a sergeant. Mr John Jardine (in the straw hat) stands next to Supt Lockton and his wife, during the 1911 celebrations.

The Callis celebrates in 1911. The village atmosphere, maintained well into this century, is very apparent here.

The Ashby Volunteers lead the parade in 1911. By 1908 they had become the 5th Battalion Leicester Regiment ('A' Company), with an armoury in (Rifle) Range Road.

A parade of nurses (above) and a field ambulance (below) passing the lower end of Market Street, possibly in 1919.

This probably shows the decorations for celebrations in 1919 to mark the end of the First World War. Note the Waverley Refreshment Rooms.

The funeral cortège of the Earl of Loudoun (1855–1920) moves down South Street.

SECTION EIGHT

Fire, Flood and Destruction

The Fire Engine House, originally in the centre of the Green, moved to the Cattle Market by 1898. Henry Morris Watts was superintendent in 1900. The building was taken down in 1979.

Ashby Fire Brigade
proudly pose by their fire
engine. Mr Randall is
behind the wheel.

The Flaxdressers' thatched roof was clearly ablaze by the time the fire brigade arrived.

A flood in 1910 makes the Smisby Road look like a canal. The railway snaked past Worthington and Breedon before finally reaching Derby.

Floods under the Callis Bridge. That's a wagon on the bridge, waiting for the Soap Works.

Elford Street railings act as a sluice for the raging Gilwiskaw.

A charabanc wades through the Derby Road in the 1925 flood.

The Baptists would have expected few in the congregation that week. The Engine House can be seen on the right.

Holdron's and Sansom's remind us that we are in Ashby and not Venice.

Water enough to provide for the tea-rooms in 1925. On Monday 18 May 'a terrific thunderstorm broke over Ashby during the afternoon' and the water was soon four feet deep in Market Street.

The town suffered again on Sunday 22 May 1932. At exactly 1.25 a.m. the Gilwiskaw overflowed its banks at the Mill Bank culvert.

Bath Street suffered the full force of the floods on both occasions. The railway embankments on Smisby Road and facing the Bath Grounds had really created two dams.

In 1925 the police station, round the corner from Ivanhoe Terrace, lost its 60-yard wall, and water was seven feet deep in places on the Bath Grounds.

The ghostly scar of a double-gabled building behind Simpkin & James' grocer's shop at 73 Market Street. The shop itself was pulled down in the 1970s.

The remnants of 11 Kilwardby Street, where Harry Haynes lived and conducted his wheelwright's business in the yard behind until the 1930s.

SECTION NINE

Great Houses, Small Houses

Cliftonthorpe – nicknamed Love's Folly, after Samuel Love (d. 1877), currier and farmer, brick, tile and sanitary pipe manufacturer, and victualler at the Queen's Head. He built the house with a tower so he could see his Market Street property.

The hall is the oldest part of the castle still standing, probably completed before 1200, but rebuilt several times since then. The roof survived until after 1730.

The Hastings Tower (originally *c.* 90 feet high) was the last major addition to the castle (*c.* 1475). To the left is the Kitchen Tower (1350–1400). Both towers were 'slighted' in 1649.

On the site of the present Manor House stood Ashby Place, for some years home of Selina, Countess of Huntingdon. The house was said to have contained seventy-one rooms. It was demolished in December 1830.

The new Manor House was built in 1831–2 by John Mammatt, steward to the Marquess of Hastings. In 1944 it was leased for additional classrooms by the Grammar School.

School House, now the Grammar School's boarding house, is probably on the site of Samuel Shaw's school, erected in the 1670s. Additions were made in 1807 and 1891.

The Mansion House in 1837 was one residence, occupied by Mrs Thornley, the widow of a rich draper of 61 Market Street. Her son owned the cottages in Hill Street and land at Hill Top. Sold after his death in 1842, the latter was soon built upon.

Highfield House was built and occupied by Mr Johnson, manager of the Leicestershire Bank. It was converted into a hotel in about 1947 but was demolished in 1971.

Built in the 1920s, St Michael's name was changed by its owner, Major Howard Smith, as being too ecclesiastical. As the Red House it was demolished in the early 1970s. The oak floor in the dining room was reputed to have come from a *Queen Mary* refit.

Willesley Hall was demolished in 1953. It was built for Sir Thomas Abney (d. 1750) on the site of an earlier house, which had been inhabited by the family since the 16th century.

Measham Hall was built by William Abney in 1767. Home to the family until the 1920s, it became the residence of the Measham Colliery managers. Because of subsidence, it was demolished in 1959.

Court no. 2, behind Hendon House in Kilwardby Street, survived until relatively recently.

Another yard, behind the New George in Market Street. As late as 1911 an Inspector's Report said: 'more than 50 per cent of the houses I visited are altogether unfit for human habitation'.

Court no. 18, at the top end of Market Street and South Street, prior to demolition. Only a few courts now remain to give a flavour of the 'wretched rookeries' Scott complained of in 1907.

SECTION TEN

Learning, Praying, Playing

In 1908 a reporter on *The Girls' Realm: A Magazine for Young Gentlewomen* commented: 'A strong team in the Midlands is the Ashby-de-la-Zouch Girls' Grammar School.'

In 1807 'a modern handsome building of two storeys' was built in South Street: the ground floor held the Classical School and the upper storey housed the English School.

Sir Joseph Hood with town dignitaries, including Tom Woodcock (third from right) and W.P. Musson (far right).

An early 20th-century photograph of the Boys' Grammar School in Leicester Road. The headmaster was Llewelyn Walter Lloyd.

Ashby Grammar School staff in the 1920s. Standing, from left: Sandy Goodwin?, George Seddon?, Jimmy Jones?, Harvey Woodward, Frank Addison?, -?-. Front row: George Scott?, -?-, Charles Elliott (headmaster), Billy Marsh, Len Matthews. (We think!)

The English School in 1906. The headmaster was Walter Ernest Jennings, who lived at 8 Rawdon Terrace; Thomas Hagger, assistant teacher, lived at 1 Old Park Villas, Nottingham Road.

The south side of the Girls' Grammar School. The site was purchased for £1,280 (in preference to buying Hill House at the top of Kilwardby Street). The single-storey building on the right held five music rooms.

Miss Ethel Mary Hogg (headmistress 1894–1907), with her staff and pupils in front of the main entrance to the new school.

The Art Room at the Girls' Grammar School. The metal staircase was only taken down in 1994 – a victim of more rigid health and safety rules.

A group of infants with Miss Wood, outside The Cottage at North Street Church of England Girls' and Infants' School.

Playtime at North Street School. The outside offices are in the background.

'There was an Old Woman . . .' outside The Cottage.

The North Street Girls' Staff 1937–8. From left: Miss Joyce Beard, Miss Gladys Underwood, Miss Ruth Hill, Mrs Wheatley, Miss Ena Kellam-Smith, Miss Annie Outram (headmistress), Miss Polly Neale, Miss Adams, Miss Bott.

The castle chapel was probably the earliest of the extensive additions made by William, Lord Hastings, between 1464 and 1483. In recent years it has been used as a mausoleum for members of the Hastings family.

The Domesday Book mentions a parish priest at Ashby; traces of 14th-century stonework can be found in the arcades leading from the chancel to the Hastings Chapel.

St Helen's was refurbished in Charles II's reign and again in 1829, and extensively enlarged in 1878–80. This 'restoration', designed by James Piers Saint Aubyn, cost over £18,000.

St Helen's Vicarage was rebuilt by the Revd John Prior (1783–1804) and further modernized by the Revd Marmaduke Vavasour (1834–75).

A rise in Ashby's population led to the building of another Anglican church, at the west end of the town. The foundation stone of Holy Trinity was laid by Earl Howe of Gopsall on 25 August 1838. The church was consecrated in 1840.

A temporary church for Roman Catholic worship had been used in Prior Park Road. The corner-stone of the present one was laid on 18 August 1913 by Robert, Bishop of Nottingham.

The Primitive Methodists built a chapel in Millbank in 1833; in 1862 they purchased the old Baptist Chapel in Mill Lane. Here the congregation meet for the last time, before moving again to New Burton Road in 1906.

In 1802 the Baptists converted a house in Mill Lane into a chapel. Inadequate accommodation led to the purchase of a site in the Cattle Market in 1862.

Wesleyan Methodists had first worshipped in a licensed building on the south side of Kilwardby Street. By 1831 a new chapel had been erected opposite; in 1869 it was rebuilt, but worship ceased there in 1958 and it was demolished *c.* 1985.

John and Charles Elliott were contractors and monumental and general masons, whose premises had been at the bottom of Wood Street since the mid-1870s.

Ashby Cottage Hospital staff 1936–7. Back row, left to right: Nurse Shillcock, Nurse Heath, Dr Davidson, Mrs Fisher Jesson, Dr Mitchell-Innes, Nurse Jones, Nurse Ransell. Front row: Nurse Goodwin, Sister Powell, Matron Arkinstall, Sister Seymour, Nurse Sharp.

The Ivanhoe Baths were not just a rendezvous for people seeking the curative effects of the waters. The Bath Grounds became a centre for recreation from the 1820s onwards.

The Ivanhoe Baths Building Orchestra in 1901. Standing, from left: Joe Curtis, Dick Grundy, Dan Kirk, -?-, Jack Tyler, Arthur Smith. Sitting: Alfred Wootton, Harry Trevor, Jack Wootton, Jimmy Owen, Ted Owen.

The North Street schoolchildren morris dancing during the 1911 maypole festivities. Miss Woods is on the far right.

The earliest record of a cricket match involving Ashby is in the *Leicester Chronicle* of September 1831, when a visiting team from Barwell won by six wickets.

Early games were played in a field near the cottage hospital. By 1880 the Ashby Hastings CC were installed on the Bath Grounds. In 1911 an offer to stage a county match there was accepted. County games continued until 1964.

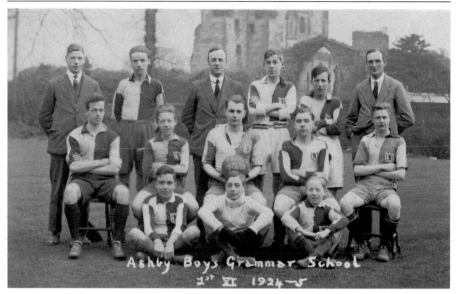

The Boys' Grammar School 1st XI. Back row, from left: Len Matthews, ? Hunt, J.E. Elliott, B. Shuttleworth, C. Wilson, H. Woodward. Middle row: B. Cheatle, S. Hurd, D. Clulow, H. Warner, E. Sankey. Front row: ? Harrison, V. Tilley, L. Orme.

Gentlemen at leisure relax by the Priest's Rooms at Ashby Castle.

SECTION ELEVEN

Blackfordby

St Margaret's, from Main Street. The Raddle Bank (recreation ground) is ahead. The cottages on the right were demolished in the mid-1960s.

Blackfordby Hall – a fine William and Mary house, home of the Joyce family for many years. It was pulled down in 1966.

On the right is one of the two timbered cottages still extant in the village. By the car is a freshwater spring, well known for its purity.

The Wesleyan Chapel, built in 1823 and enlarged in 1860, seated 150 people. It was converted into a house in the 1930s and demolished in the mid-1960s.

The earliest known photograph of village Methodists, outside Sunbeam Cottage, Butt Lane.

Blackfordby Boys' Brigade.

The official opening of the new Methodist Chapel in the 1930s.

The village football club, 1910–11.

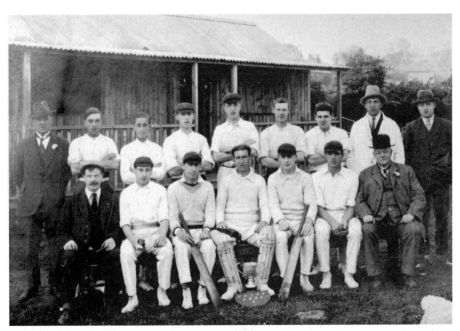

Blackfordby Cricket Club – winners of the John Knowles Hassall Cup in 1923.
Standing, from left: P. Hall, G. Adams, H. Martin, J. Farmer, R. Hall, T. Illsley, S. Smith,
W. Timms (umpire), S. Henney. Front row: I. Timms (scorer), J. Timms, T. Hulme (vice-
capt.), C. Hackett (capt.), H. Orme, S. Hulme, J. Illsley.

A village gathering around a huge tree on the recreation ground, which was felled in 1927 after being declared unsafe.

The first National School, built in 1843, later known as the 'Stute (Institute), where village functions were held. It is now used by the Youth Club.

Blackfordby School, built in 1889, had two playgrounds (one for boys, one for girls). The headmaster's house was far left.

Mr and Mrs Jenkins, the first headmaster of the new school, and his wife. This retirement photograph was given to every pupil.

Norris Hill, built in 1845 by Henry Brown, an Ashby solicitor and farmer. In June 1928, at the Royal Hotel, Ashby, Mr Blakesley bought this 'charming freehold country residence'.

Mr Gilbert Hutchinson, who owned and lived at Norris Hill (1921–8) showing one of his prize shires.

SECTION TWELVE

Packington

Bridge Street, showing the bridge built by the Abney-Hastings over the Gilwiskaw.

Packington High Street, looking towards the present post office, with the blacksmith's and Methodist Church on the left.

Looking up the High Street, past Little Lane, with Grange Farm on the right and Hill Farm on the left.

Two of the Nixon children pose near the village Reading Room.

Packington lock-up is octagonal, and has a brick octagonal spire with a ball on top. It stands next to the Pinfold and was used as an ARP Wardens' Post in the Second World War. The cottages have gone.

Holy Rood, Packington, probably stands on the site of a pre-Conquest foundation. The earliest parts of the church date from the 13th century.

The Revd Arthur Mammatt (vicar of Packington 1890–1901), his wife Katherine, and his sons Martin (b. 1888) and Gerald (b. 1889).

Packington School teachers at the vicarage. From left: Miss E. Spare, Miss A. Bott (with parasol), Miss M. Kinns and Miss E. Peach.

The 1922 school photograph, with Miss Martha Oakey on the left and Miss Mary Swann on the right.

Packington Baptist Chapel in Mill Lane, closed in 1948 and demolished in 1950.

Packington Mill was one of four water mills within a couple of miles on the Gilwiskaw. It ceased working in 1947, when the dam banks broke. It is mentioned in the Domesday Book.

SECTION THIRTEEN

Smisby and Coleorton

Coleorton almshouses, built on the site of the old Beaumont endowed school, were rebuilt by Sir George Beaumont in 1867.

St James' Church, Smisby. From the tower, Sir Walter Scott is said to have conceived the idea of the tournament which figured in his famous novel *Ivanhoe*.

The Smisby lock-up was built in 1790, immediately after a court order from the quarter sessions. It is an octagonal structure and is still a prominent feature of the village.

A view of Smisby from St James' tower.

Main Street, Smisby. The footpath to the Nelson inn is by the bicycle.

Two further views of Smisby, redolent of the early years of this century. In 1901 the population was 325, having decreased by 90 since 1851.

A view from the main Derby–Ashby road into Main Street.

Forty Lane, unchanged today. It is clearly a very ancient track.

Coleorton Hall was planned in 1800 and completed in 1807 by Sir George Beaumont (7th baronet). Few houses in England have richer literary and artistic memories, for there are links with Wordsworth and Sir Walter Scott.

Coleorton School, founded in 1701 by Viscount Beaumont, was rebuilt on this site by Canon William Beresford Beaumont in 1867.

St Mary the Virgin, Coleorton, built in the Gothic style. The spire was struck by lightning in 1839 and severely damaged.

The old village lay on the north-western side of the parish, close to the 13th-century church. This group of cottages is on the old Loughborough Road.

Did you hear
we are leaving Ashby-de-la-Zouch

Acknowledgements

I wish, in some ways, this book had been gathered together twenty years ago – many more people would have been alive to reminisce about the Ashby of the 1880s onwards. I have been fortunate in talking to Old Ashbeians since I first came to the town in 1978, but I now realize the conversations were too few in number. For all that, I remember with gratitude and abiding interest my chats with 'Bev' and Hilda Gilbert (née Trevor), Sidney Staynes (Litherland's), William and Eddie Arnold, Daisy Foster, Sam Lathbury, Dick Fenning, Gladys Howell, Joe Richards, Lawrence Tipton and others no longer with us.

Len Matthews (ninety-nine this year), the Misses Joan and Selina Smedley, Miss Eva Belton, Ken Mackay, Robert Jones, David Jackson, Vernon Smith, Laura and Peter Cooper, and Christopher Bailey have all been most helpful with identifying and commenting on the pictures. Most of the above, as well as Mrs Jennifer Pilgrim, Gerald Wright and Arthur Mammatt, have kindly lent me photographs or postcards. I take full responsibility for any mistakes, however! My final thanks is, as always, to Christine, Kirsty and Stuart for letting me have the time to do the research.